THE SAINTS

IN

DAILY CHRISTIAN LIFE

A PROJECT OF DIMENSION BOOKS

THE SAINTS
IN DAILY CHRISTIAN LIFE

BY ROMANO GUARDINI

235.2
G93

CHILTON BOOKS — A DIVISION OF THE CHILTON COMPANY
Publishers   PHILADELPHIA AND NEW YORK

Published by Dimension Books, Wilkes-Barre, Pennsylvania in association with Chilton Books and simultaneously in Toronto, Canada by Ambassador Books, Ltd.

Nihil Obstat
P.M-D. Forestier

Imprimatur
Paris, 5 Janvier 1965
J. Hottot, V.G.

Library of Congress Catalog Card Number: 66-17193

Copyright © 1966 by Dimension Books

CONTENTS

PUBLISHER'S NOTE

The following pages give us important observations by one of the most distinguished Catholic theologians alive on questions urgently debated in the recent Vatican Council. They also shed light on matters of somewhat wider scope: questions with which the Council did not deal but which have interested theologians and spiritual writers as well as the laity in general throughout the Christian world. Ever since the appearance of Romano Guardini's **The Lord,** we have learned to look to him for brief, clear, non-technical explanation of religious questions that are close to us, and which have practical meaning in terms of daily Catholic life. His suggestions in this work about "a new kind of saint" demanded by our times as well as his treatment of sanctity and the laity will prove most stimulating.

Booksellers, librarians, writers, and specialists in religious publishing have often complained quite bitterly of the phantom-like, saccharine perspective in which saints' lives are presented to the public. Perhaps Professor Guardini's book will have a beneficial influence in this respect too: his sketch of the meaning and development of sanctity inside Christian history gives both realism and vigor to an area in which both elements are unfortunately often lacking.

Professor Guardini's book is the introductory volume to one of the major Catholic publishing projects of our time: **The Encyclopedia of Catholic Saints.** This is an all-new, fully-updated library of information about the lives and activities of every saint celebrated in the Catholic liturgy. The treatment will not be alphabetical as in a dictionary, but will follow the living worship of the Church with a day-by-day and month-by-month treatment in twelve volumes. To the more than one hundred fifty collaborators whose energy and devotion have now made possible the international publication of this project, a special word of thanks is necessary. Their work was inspired and guided by a distinguished panel of editors and writers whose celebrated names gave much greater meaning to the whole work: Francois Mauriac, Pere

PUBLISHER'S NOTE

Jean Danielou, Gustave Thibon, Daniel-Rops, Romano Guardini, Robert Morel, Michel Quoist, Joseph Delteil, Msgr. Charles Journet, Ida Goerres, Pere Paul Doncoeur and Pere Chenu. To these latter, whose courage and foresight brought us through many difficulties that might otherwise have been insurmountable, thanks alone is insufficient. May they find satisfaction in viewing a work already praised throughout the world by historians and theologians to be among the most brilliant and challenging Catholic publications of our time.

FOREWARD

JEAN BAPTISTE HENRI LACORDAIRE

A saint is not simply the point of confluence, the meeting of all the Christian virtues in one and the same soul. This is but ordinary sanctity, that which is necessary to the salvation of every Christian. There is no Christian in the state of union with God in whom humility, chastity, and charity do not meet together in a degree more or less perfect. We call such people pious men; we might even, to speak widely, call them saints; but this is not what we understand by that great expression **-the saints!** What then are the saints? What then is sanctity thus understood?

Sanctity is the love of God and of men carried to a sublime extravagance. If communion between the Infinite and the finite really exists; if the heart of God creates a dwelling and lives in the heart of man, it is impossible, at least in certain souls more ardent than the rest, that the presence of an element so prodigious should not become visible, should not produce extraordinary effects which the weakness of our nature and of our language would constrain us to call extravagant. For what is the meaning of this word? It means **that which goes beyond.**

There is in sanctity a phenomenon of extravagance, a love of God and men which frequently defies ordinary human understanding. But this is not the unique characteristic of sanctity; extravagance alone would be only singularity, and singularity proves nothing in favor of the man who makes it a part of his actions, if it is not perhaps a great deal of vanity and a little of bad education. Extravagance in sanctity should be corrected by another element, and it is in fact by the **sublime** -that is to say, by moral beauty in its highest degree; by that beauty which causes the rapture of human sense. Thus, there is in sanctity something which wounds human sense and something which enraptures it; something which produces stupor and something which produces ad-**miration.**

And these two things are not separated there, like two streams which flow side by side. But the extravagant and the sublime, that which wounds human sense and that which enraptures it, mingled and dissolved the one with the other, make of sanctity but one tissue, in which it is impossible for the most active spirit of analysis, at the moment when it sees the saint in action, to distinguish that which is extravagant from that which is sublime — that which binds man to earth from that which lifts him up even to God.

Defining sanctity in these terms, we would naturally expect the history of the saints to be a rare phenomenon, reserved to one time or to one country. But the truth is the exact opposite. It is a general and a constant phenomenon. Wherever Catholic doctrine takes root, even where (so to speak) it is placed as a grain of seed between rocks, sanctity appears and becomes manifest in some souls by fruits which defy the esteem and the scorn of reason. That sublime extra-

vagance dates from a yet higher and more unutterable folly — the folly described by Saint Paul of a God dying upon a Cross, His head crowned with thorns, His feet and His hands pierced, His body bruised and mutilated. Since that time the contagion of holiness has never ceased to choose victims in the world — victims to whom belong the heritage of the cross, the living tradition of voluntary martyrdom, the dignity of extravagance and the glory of the sublime.

THE SAINTS IN DAILY CHRISTIAN LIFE

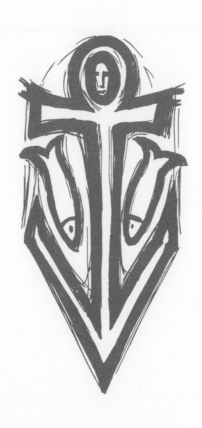

WHAT IS A SAINT

Most of the dates on our calendar bear the name of some great person in Christian history. That person is generally reputed to have had a certain distinctive character — such as that of a dynamic apostle like St. Paul or that of holiness and poverty as in the case of St. Francis or that of abandonment to Divine Providence as in the lives of great mystics like John of the Cross and Teresa of Avila. Almost everyone, believer or not, regards these persons as venerable, as worthy of respect.

But in addition, if we happen to be believers, they are still more important; for us who believe, they are a reminder as well as a promise of our future glory. We rejoice when we come upon their faces in Christian art; when their names occur in legend and poetry; or when we reflect quite simply that it is their names which we ourselves bear throughout life.

But what is it that at root constitutes a Saint? Just what kind of people are these Saints?

A FIRST ANSWER

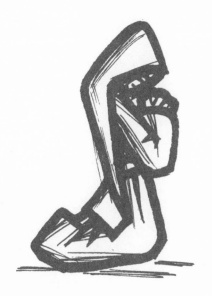

One needs to familiarize oneself with the saints just a bit to find one obvious and easy answer. The Jewish people were told in the Old Testament of a commandment which Jesus Christ Himself later called "the first and the greatest," and which He enjoined upon all His followers without exception:

> "You shall love the Lord, your God, with all your heart and with all your soul and with all your strength."
> (Deut. 6:5; Matt. 22:37)

Viewed in this perspective, a saint is simply a man to whom God has given the strength to take this primal commandment with utter seriousness, to understand it profoundly, and to bend every effort to carry it out.

The importance of this divine command cannot be exaggerated — it is something overarching all religious experience and activity; something, in the proper sense, awful. Just consider the reorientation of life, the purpose, the energy and ambition which must possess the man who accepts it. All this in part serves to explain that reverential fear which we believers feel when we contemplate the lives of the

saints, and also the mysterious attraction which their lives will continue to exercise upon us to the end of our days.

The Saints, then, are men and women who go forward to meet God's command resolutely and completely, without reservation. This description of a saint is valid for all of them, among all peoples and in all times.

But this is not an entirely satisfactory description. It tells us very little about the modalities in which men love God, or about the way in which a likeness to the saints should be reflected in the Christian conscience today. Basically, of course, sanctity is concerned with the development of charity, and there is no difference between a saint of ancient and modern times in this regard. But the manner in which the unfolding of charity manifests itself in the course of history — that is different, and it is that which we must determine if we are to grasp the relation of the saints to current society.

THE SAINTS IN THE NEW TESTAMENT

Saint Paul was the great witness to the Christian life in its beginnings, and his words will always remain a great watershed of truth about any religious question that concerns us. But if we inquire in his writings for an explanation of the meaning of sanctity, his ideas seem at first quite strange. Read, for instance, his salutation at the opening of his Second Epistle to the Corinthians:

> "Paul, an Apostle of Jesus Christ by the will of God, and Timothy our brother, to the Church of God that is at Corinth, with all the saints that are in the whole of Achaia . . . "

And at the end of the same Epistle we read:

> "All the saints send you greetings;"

the saints in this reference are the people of the country from which the Apostle is writing, Macedonia.

What could Paul have meant by his use of the word "saints" in these passages. Evidently and plainly, he was referring to the Christians, and to all of them; to those who received the Good News, who confessed the Christian faith and who were reborn in baptism to a new life. Accordingly, he intended something different by the word "saints" than we ourselves do. When we speak of saints, we think of those great individuals of Christianity whose solemn figures are found in our Churches. But here is Saint Paul, speaking of people who live out their lives at Corinth, at Thessalonica and at Ephesus; who believe, who hope, who struggle against their weaknesses in the spiritual order and who from the standpoint of religious history do not seem to be extraordinary in any way.

What then constituted for Paul the special character designated by the word Saint?

First of all we should appreciate the fact that in the early days of the Church it was something quite remarkable just to become a Christian, just to try to live as a Christian. If a man made up his mind to become a Christian, he tore himself loose from a whole skein of practices and habits and social customs that identified his life up to that point. He became a stranger even to his closest friends; and if his family did not join him in his conversion, he was frequently rejected by them, separated from them forever.

In Roman and Greek antiquity, moreover, the whole of life was permeated with pagan customs. Language was filled with illusions to the gods, to myths; the manner of life differed entirely from that which the Christian considered a matter of obligation. It was a painful thing to become a Christian — it involved misunderstanding, troubles, difficulties without number. Religious celebrations of the community, altogether brilliant in many cases and become a matter of intense sentiment for the average citizen, were forbidden to the convert. Since the ceremonies of the city and the state were bound up with the national gods, it was impossible for the Christian to participate in them. Either that, or else he had to maintain a very difficult reserve — one which required as much renunciation as it did wisdom. In matters dealing with the State, which considered itself to be divine just as the Emperor viewed himself as a high priest, it was inevitable that the Christian should get into troublesome predicaments. He thus found himself sharply at odds with the public law and the local courts.

Whoever became a Christian undertook, then, a course burdened with terrible consequences. He entered upon a life in which he had frequently to defy his friends, to swim in a sea of renunciation, and to look forward to eventual imprisonment, persecution or even death. In this light it is not hard to understand why Paul would refer to the early Christians as saints.

But there is yet something else, and this is the main point. The people of early Christian times really understood what it was to be a pagan. They knew from their own experience the limitations of paganism — how in spite of its great culture and refinement, one remained a prisoner of the forces of nature; how despite the fantastic intellectual and artistic achievements of paganism, it offered little consolation to the distressed and lonely human heart; how, the beautiful poetic myths and fables of paganism notwithstanding, relatively little was done to satisfy the profound human aspiration for truth and liberty.

In Christianity, people of ancient times encountered for the first time grandeur, Good News. They experienced the profound meaning of matters to which we have become so accustomed that we are almost blind to their greatness:

"Christ's love which surpasses all knowledge" (Eph. 3:19), the story of the hundredth sheep for which the Good Shepherd ceaselessly searches, the Bread which is given for the life of the world. And they were learning what it is to grow every day in the new life of the Kingdom of God. They were, quite simply, living a new kind of existence ruled by the God who was also their King and their Saint; the apostle thus had the right to call them saints themselves.

SAINTS OF THE EXCEPTIONAL WAY

As time went on and Christians became more numerous, the quality and seriousness of their faith frequently suffered diminution. In addition, there were more and more children among the newly baptized; these children were seldom aware of the immense scope of the act of baptism, and consequently viewed as quite natural things that were of themselves extraordinary — in fact supernatural.

After the conversion of the Emperor Constantine, Christianity was even more seriously threatened by the fact that it became a state religion. If a man wanted to be considered a good citizen, if he wanted to obtain public advancement, he had to be a Christian, at least in name and in public deportment. We can easily imagine to what extent Christian life as a whole was thereby debased, became externalized, found its main energies and intentions obscured. Under these conditions, it was no longer possible to speak of all Christians as Saints.

As a result, a new concept of sanctity developed. People began to consider the saint as a person who fulfilled the "great commandment" to an extraordinary degree.

It was especially the Martyr, the person who gave his life for the faith, who was exalted in this setting. Men such as Stephen or Ignatius, women like Perpetua or Agnes were crowned with the glory of Christian heroism. Their death alone rendered them worthy of special homage.

There were other ways too of expressing what Lacordaire calls the "extravagance of sanctity," of revealing a personal and unbounded love of God.

One man would experience such a profound horror of sin that he was not satisfied simply to repent, to make amends. He would break off with his entire society, go into utter solitude like Antony of the Desert and lead there a life of penance whose rigor even after twenty centuries still makes us shudder.

Another, moved by "the treasures of heaven" spoken of in the Gospel or by the riches of union with God would embrace an ultimate poverty: this is what Francis and Clare did, and to such a degree that even the secular world recounts after centuries their greatness.

Still more, gripped in their inner beings by the commandment to love their neighbors, consecrated themselves to the service of the poor and the sick. Let us simply recall Elizabeth of Hungary washing the feet of lepers, or Vincent de Paul and the Sisters of Charity.

Others, overwhelmed by the grandeur of the revealed word, lived only to study it, to break the bread of truth to their brothers, like Anselm of Canterbury or Thomas Aquinas.

Last but not least, many heard in their hearts the words of Christ: "Go, therefore, and make disciples of all nations" (Matt. 28:19), and were set on fire with apostolic zeal to carry Christ's message to the world, sometimes even to seal their words with their blood: Patrick in Ireland, Boniface in Germany, Francis Xavier in the Far East.

Such is the inexhaustible "proliferation of graces and vocations" of which Saint Paul spoke in the early Church.

The lives of these saints are diverse, but always of an extraordinary character. They come from all levels of society: kings and peasants, knights and artisans, women, men, young people, children even. But they all have one thing in common: the demands which the love of God makes upon their hearts causes them to transcend the ordinary mass of human beings and to accomplish something altogether exceptional.

This alone make them witnesses of the eternally new greatness which Christ alone has made possible in history. They refract, so to speak, the light of divine simplicity into forms of infinite variety. They are the models, they show the aims and the paths of sanctity, they arouse the forces which will continue to work for centuries, their lives describe the outlines of which other Christians will simply fill in the details with imitation and accomplishment.

Such is the idea of the Saint which has dominated the Christian conscience up to our times. This idea will doubtless remain valid for all times — not only because it is true but because our daily life has need of heroes, of great figures in whom the power of divine grace is clearly manifested and whose magnificence surpasses all that is earthly.

Dominic, Augustine or Ignatius, King Louis of France, Empress Cunegonda, the slave Notburga, The peasant Nicolas of Flue will always remain resplendent witnesses to what love can do when it surpasses all bounds. They are the figures of Christian heroism which is expressed in a life of boldness, in a life that knows no holding-back, no reserve, but only patience and dynamic action.

A NEW KIND OF SAINT

In our day the idea of a Saint appears to be undergoing a new and signficant transformation. It seems that the notion of something exceptional or extravagant is no longer necessarily involved in the meaning of the word saint.

The evidence for this view is muliform, but the best way to approach a complete understanding of it seems to be through the writing of an 18th century spiritual writer, Jean Pierre de Caussade, who wrote books of simple and vigorous meditation intended primarily for religious, but one of interest to the laity too, provided only they make the necessary transpositions. In his main work, entitled **On Abandonment to Divine Providence,** a Christian who wishes to become a saint asks the question: **What kind of life must I lead?** To this

Caussade answers: "You must not make any particular plans, but do only what each hour, each minute demands of you. It is God Himself in His Providence who looks out for you. The road to sanctity does not follow a preconceived system of actions and exercises, but travels the very complicated fabric of life itself. Progress in the spiritual life does not consist so much in achievement, in actual accomplishment, as in a greater and greater purity of love with which you do at each moment what the situation demands. Note that you

must do what it really demands; not what selfish motives might desire, what personal preference or convenience or advantage or pleasure might dictate. It is the situation itself which speaks with the voice of God and which says 'This is necessary, you must help this person, you must do this work, you must show patience under this trial . . .' " To do all this, strictly, without excuses and without reservations, and with no effort to reap anything by way of personal desire or to lessen or falsify things for the sake of escape — that, says Caussade, leads to sanctity.

The same book of Caussade deals with the question: **How does one go about loving God?** He comments at the outset on the common experience of all who have had the slightest glimmer of religious experience: it is easy to love God, or to think one does so, when God's presence to us is something emotional or sentimental. Love under these circumstances is a very natural thing, penetrating the depths of the soul. But this is not generally the case with religious people. Most of the time our hearts are at one extreme or the other: quiet or else in rebellion. Daily life with its anxieties

and bustle smothers everything, or else overly exerts us. What then is love? Precisely this: "to do what is to be done in the present moment, because it is exactly that which fulfills the will of God. And to do it as charity should be performed, in a spirit of purity and good will."

This is the love of which our Lord spoke, and which He said must be with **all our heart and all our soul and all our strength** — but who can ever say that he acts thus? That all his heart, all his soul, all his strength have really been put into any action? If we were only to act in this way but once, we would immediately sense the almost unlimited possibilities for progress that are latent in the world and in ourselves. There are possibilities in us which could lead us ever farther, out beyond the horizons, to a place where we would have to start over and over again the process of clarifying our intentions, removing after-thoughts and shedding light on interior dodges and dishonesties, conquering the rebellion and meannesses in our hearts. These are the possibilities of which Christ has spoken in His "All": all the heart, all the soul, all

the strength. But what can this "all" possibly mean when it concerns the infinite and all-holy God who sees everything, and whose love it is in the first place which makes ours possible?

If we were to probe a little further into the answer to this question, we would be able to recognize the outlines of the figure of a new type of saint. It is no longer a matter of a man or woman who does exceptional things, but simply of one who does what every man and woman who wishes to act well in a given situation will do. No more, and no less.

Above all, however, this man acts in the perspective of God's will. He understands that the task which presents itself to him here and now is indeed something which he must accomplish. He is not a visionary, neither is he a slouch. He makes use of his intelligence to do his duty before God and can give a good reason at all times for what he does. But more important still, his conscience has experienced a great deepening. His actions are placed in the world, but are subject to the will of God who is the Creator of the world and yet in His Infinity outside it. In the midst of a life disjointed by all sorts of selfishness and lies, he is in search of a primal innocence which marked it in the beginning before man set himself at odds with God.

To desire these things: that is true love. And in that love, let us repeat, there are limitless possibilities: that of a truth which is always to be more complete, of good always to be made more pure, of action always to be more resolute. To see in these beginnings the all of which our Lord speaks: all of the heart, all of the soul, all of the strength; to be able to see all in these humble beginnings: it is that in which sanctity consists. And this sanctity grows in the continuing struggles

against oneself: in the necessary renunciations, in the challenging effort toward an ever purer sincerity of spirit and intention.

THE SAINTS IN OUR WORLD

Sanctity nurtured in this way is less and less an obvious thing. One could almost say that this is a deliberately hidden sanctity: one that hides its greatness, one that does things of lesser and lesser importance **rightly;** but by that fact they become of greater and greater significance.

Of less importance: for what he does is no longer important, be it great, difficult, or dangerous — these things do not finally matter. What is demanded of us may be something challenging or something only very average or even minimal. It does not matter. It is needful only that it is done right. But on the other hand, **of greater signficance:** because the actions required are performed in the manner absolutely necessary for each of them, not as personal considerations or feelings might dictate, but in the manner desired by God who has created all things and whose will speaks in each situation by the fact that the situation is as it is.

Man receives his task in life from the hand of God — from the God who is truth and who has no interest in dissemblers or fakers or those who wish to leave a job half-done. Each action of man takes on significace in that it is more than man, more even than God, but a concurrence between the man who acts and God who in that precise moment places his Creation in man's hands — as he did with the first man, "to till it and to keep it" (Gen. 2:15). What happens in this perspective is most singular: the object of the action appears much more distinctly and clearly in its essence, for what it is, and at the same time by its very objectivity infused with greater meaning in that it is done for God. There is nothing extravagant, nothing extraordinary or brilliant: there is no question here of great experiences, of dangers boldly encountered or of dazzling breakthroughs. It is hardly a matter of anything of any consequqence at all —

except, and it is in this that its signficance lies, it is a person who acts with God, and for God. There is nothing to call attention to the person. We might even work beside such a person, walk with him, and note nothing special. But the man whose spirit is attuned to see these things will notice a quiet freedom, a calm assurance, a spirit of love and orientation to the divine, a heart that remains joyous of all cares and trials.

If what we have thus far suggested be true, or at least capable of further elaboration toward the truth, then we can possibly sketch from it the figure of a new type of Saint — one who will be closer to the spirit and character of our age. Our times appear to be distrustful of extraordinary personalities and of heroes, of supermen. This is true in spite of the unhealthy, even insensate fascination still shown

by some for the sensational in books and movies. People today revere the sincere, the authentic, the genuine, the real far above that which pretends to be superhuman or heroic. Let me cite just two instances of what I mean.

Toward the end of the first world war the expression "unknown soldier" began to appear in everyday use. Formerly we spoke of great generals, of great commanders and admirals who performed glorious deeds on land and sea. Such people began to lose their fascination on the popular mind and were replaced, significantly, by average

people who love their country, who know their duty and do it, who act calmly and decisively right where they happen to be.

In another order something analogous has taken place. In technical, scientific or social tasks like those of space exploration or politics, the complexities of the work itself has caused the individual to be replaced by teams, by work-groups in which no one person can gain any special distinction apart from the others but where each is important.

Each man does his own job but also shares responsibility for the total and common project. Each knows that he can have confidence in the others as far as the project itself is concerned. As far as labor and achievement are concerned, each is equal.

In such instances as these we observe what we may call the retreat of the extraordinary from the stage of history as well as from the main consideration of people today. The individual effaces himself but in return gains a new importance in his sharpened awareness of the social dimension of his task and its benefit to his society.

It does not seem improper to compare what is happening on these human and natural levels with what goes on in the supernatural order of sanctity. The saint will no longer be characterized by extraordinary behavior (as the historian, say, understands it); he will no longer appear to the world as separated from his fellow men or above them. On

the contrary, he will be doing the same thing as everyone else: what needs to be done, what is right and just. But he will join to his behavior a purity of intention more and more deeply united to a great love of God; more and more detached from selfishness and self-satisfaction. He thus attains a freedom which has nothing to do with great originality or genius, but only with his tremendously simple status as a person.

This is not to deny that each man will always have a particular task in the general plan of history which God is carrying out in the world. As the world becomes increasingly complex, however, more and more tasks will await us as we put ourselves at God's disposal. They will be numerous and important, but they should never be allowed to overshadow our grandeur as human persons. Reflect for a moment on the power which modern man has achieved over nature, but see too how it is outdistancing him and turning back against him vengefully at every corner because he has forgotten his personal life; or think of how the individual is today absorbed by the state and society until he no longer thinks of himself as any more than the number issued to him, as a file in some governmental bureaucrat's desk.

To appreciate the grandeur of the person, one must of course have faith. **But can an honest man still believe today?** And not merely "still believe," just that, but believe with a faith that is fully conscious and responsible? How is such a faith formed? In the first Epistle of the Apostle John, we read this phrase:

"This is the victory that overcomes the world, our faith." (Jo. 5:4)

The world exerts its pressure on us: externally in a thousand ways, but in many more and with much greater insistence internally. It acts on the circumstances and pre-conditions of our thoughts, on the criteria of our judgment, on our perception of what is real and what is essential. It assails us from all sides and tries to overwhelm us entirely. If the world succeeds, we can no longer believe. We must then overcome this pressure of the world, must free our minds and hearts and spirits, must move further away from it each day.

Admittedly, this has always been the Christian's task. But its nature has changed from period to period. It is very instructive to meditate on what it was in early Christian times, when the world was dominated by myth; in the middle ages when the problem was trying to bring order out of the chaos resulting from the great invasions; and in modern times, where the great enthusiasm of the individual giving himself back to God set itself against the outbreak of individualism. Each time there was a victory. An intuition beginning in the heart and in the spirit, a choice made deep

within the person gave a new form to the relationship between the believer and the world.

The time has come for this to be done again: for the world to be once more "overcome," so that we may have a living faith. It is no longer a question of "still believing," of individuals belonging by their inclinations to bygone times, of fighting over and over again the religious battles of the past. Nor can faith close its eyes to the reality of the world as it is today and lead an artificial life in a private preserve. Still less should we accept the irrational resolution (advocated by Kierkegaard and other philosophers) to leap toward God in blindness and despair, even though (according to this view) it is impossible ever to find him. All these attitudes are things of the past, and we are obliged today to find a new way toward the truth.

Let me suggest one way in which we might do this.

The world is closing up more and more tightly on us. For many, the world is felt to be the unique, the only reality — a "nature" whose existence has no need of just-ification or cause, a thing which is sufficient unto itself. To cope with this attitude we should know how to examine it from a new viewpoint. We must learn how to distinguish in a new way the forms, the relations of the world. We must see — and not just think nor affirm but see with our eyes — that the world is not really a "nature" as the monists describe it, but the handiwork of God; that it is not a self-sufficient universe, but a word that speaks to us of God; and that man is not imprisoned by external or internal forces but can achieve real liberty. Obviously it is not a question here of discovering some secret gap in the coherence of nature or the real; of opening a window in the wall, but of seeing that the world is a countenance through which God looks at us. In the light of that look, we will be capable of having the freedom of the sons of God.

We are not searching any longer for something garish or loud or sensational. On the contrary, we have to discover again the silent, the delicate, the tender. These are the things which can transfigure life. But they can come into the heart and the spirit only when we place ourselves at God's disposal.

This is the main area for a true understanding of which we look to the new saints for our instruction. And here is another one: that they show us today how to cultivate a love which is stronger than brute force and political power. We must look to them too for new miracles. (Some say that there is no such thing as a miracle, or at least there are none today: the surprising thing about this assertion is that it is nearly always uttered by people who have a truly astounding confidence in the most bizarre forms of fakery and charlatanism in the medical, social, cultural and political fields.) The new miracles will not be different than the old, in the sense that they are anything else than a manifestion of divine power in reality. But they will be different in mode, just as God's method of appearance varies according to the historical moment. Perhaps the greatest miracle we can expect is to see lightened the crushing burden of a world from which people feel they have no escape, in which they can find no solace, in which they are driven this way and that with frenzy and despair; perhaps the greatest miracle of all would be the discovery by our society in the saints the peace of Christ which surpasses all understanding.

SANCTITY AND THE LAITY

The sanctity of which we have just spoken — a sanctity which withdraws more and more into the background as it becomes more and more intense — relates particularly to the role of the laity, whose position in the Church is the subject of such urgent discussion today. What kind of saints will lay people be?

Not certainly the saints of the exceptional, for whose existence there must in general be an atmosphere favoring the extraordinary. The latter no longer exists for believers today. Their surroundings are standardized: they work in laboratories, in factories, in administrative a g e n c i e s and organizations which function in a predetermined way; they live in homes which are often the same to the slightest detail; they dress the same, and are subject to uniform "packages" of education, entertainment, legislation. In such an environment, how could they lead a Christian way of life which had to express itself in extraordinary religious practices and experiences? They would have to become strangers to their own ways of existence; they themselves would have to recognize their lives as absurdities. Or else they would tell themselves that sanctity is not for them, but reserved for people in a world apart, people especially prepared for it. And in this latter instance, what would have to be done with our Lord's teaching:

> "You therefore are to be perfect, even as your
> heavenly father is perfect." (Matt. 5:48)

There is a way of sanctity open to all. It is a way entangled in many theological problems, some of which touch

the very roots of Christian life. But it is one in which we can locate at least some clear ideas. It is a way founded on the premise that the laity is answerable for the world.

From the time of the middle ages, but increasingly so in modern times, Christian peoples have been developing an idea of revolutionary significance—namely, that religion is not simply the private relationship of a man or woman with God but also involves the right ordering and developing of the world. We might say that a religious character was stamped upon the world in the techniques of industry, in the improvements of the sciences, in the evolution of political life, insofar as all these relate back to the improvement of the world before God. The idea of altering the world for God's sake is so deep-rooted and pervasive that we might almost overlook it. It is also new and shattering in terms of the pagan history that preceded it, this tremendous idea of Crea-

tion being filled by man with the thought of God and of man accomplishing the duty God has given for the world.

Of course this is not really a new idea; people had only forgotten it. It has always been a first article of the faith that God is the Father of the world. But for many centuries the idea had ceased being active in man's consciousness. In that time the world was regarded as profane, neutral, autonomous.

And even after the idea was restored to man, it was never unopposed; it was not unopposed in the past, any more than it is a dominant and controlling idea of all society today. We have the proclamations of positivism to contend with now; we have the programs of totalitarian states; and we have within us, in our Christian consciences, weaknesses and frailities that pose still greater danger to a vibrant Christianity. We can neglect our duties, just as we can accept a disembodied, phanton-like piety from which the thought of transforming the world for God remains absent.

In the past few generations, the latter type of devotion has to some extent displaced the notion that the world is a task God has given us, retarded a fuller development of

the idea of world as God's property for which man is answerable.

But man is still answerable for the world, and the world is entrusted to man. He is charged with seeing that all goes well — to the extent that this is possible after sin and its many disorders. Each man has this responsibility, at that exact point in space and time where he is. His mission is not a "profane" task paralleling the religious one. It is of itself and as such religious or rather Christian. In the final analysis there is one obedience, one service which man owes God in his faith and in his work.

We think all too little of our "mission." We are too little aware of the world as the work of God, work loved by him, work that is "good." Open the pages of the Old Testament to see the phrase repeated five times in the account of Creation: "And God saw that it was good" (Gen. 1). It is this

world which is good before God that is entrusted to God. Too often religious people speak glibly of the world as a dirty place, as a sphere subject to the dominion of evil and seduction.

One consequence of this latter view is that the world has fallen prey to incredulity: I don't refer here only to those outside the faith but also to people of the Church who do their daily work not from a sense of responsibility to the faith but only out of their technical competence or for the sake of personal advantage. This secularization of work is at root one of the greatest dangers man faces in our time: spurred on by some blind belief in an inevitable progress, he thinks that the world can run itself, that human energy is sufficient to itself without the direction and staying-power of the faith. But the faith must take the world in hand to give it order, liberty and balance which are essential to dominate the chaos on whose brink civilization continually totters. This does not (we should note) take away anything from the professionalism of the scholars, the engineers, the artists, the politicians. It merely elevates their technical capacities to a higher order; it gives them more ultimate meaning and harmony with man's whole life and destiny.

None of these observations on the sanctity of the layman's role should be understood to suggest any of the rather wild notions that the laymen is a priest, or a pontiff or anything of that sort. Certain theologians, reading in Peter's Epistle about the "holy priesthood" of the laity, have spread about some ill-formed notions on the role of the laity. Only confusion has resulted. The layman is not a priest, not even in an attenuated or symbolic manner. His mission, his responsibility have nothing to do with those of the priest, and they cannot be derived from them. His role derives at root from the second chapter of Genesis where, after the account of creation, God gives the world to man in the form of a paradise for him "to till it and to keep it" (Gen. 2:15).

This paradise is not a world of imagination or of fable. It is the real world, the work of the hands of God, sharing in the relation to grace which God has given man. God has established the latter as master of the world. But man's sovereignty is really a service; and the service succeeds to the extent that man fulfills it in purity. For real sovereignty is not violence but truth. This truth consists in seeing the essence of things and doing them justice for what they are: the handiwork of God, which is to be given back to God.

This paradise is not a world of imagination or of fable. It is the real world, the work of the hands of God, sharing in the relation to grace which God has given man. God has established the latter as master of the world. But

man's sovereignty is really a service; and the service succeeds to the extent that man fulfills it in purity. For real sovereignty is not violence but truth. The truth consists in seeing the essence of things and doing them justice for what they are:

the handiwork of God, which is to be given back to God.

Man's revolt destroyed to a certain extent the paradise which God gave him. Sin clouded his vision and rendered his sovereignty uncertain. But the world continues and redemption has raised all things to new, undreamed of possibilities. To understand the world from this point of view, to see how life has been harmed by sin, to set out to give it form, to make a work of it, to start in motion the good things in man's heart, to make fresh beginnings in spite of repeated failures — that is the mission of the Christian layman today. Instead of being the master of the world, man must now struggle tragically just to bring order to a life that is in revolt. That is where he must prove himself.

What criterion can be applied to judge man's achievement? First and most important of all, man must be judged by his dutiful accomplishment of the work given him, the work necessary for the world. It is one thing to worry about our good intentions, to think about whether we are conscientious or honest. But we must first of all do the things that the world expects of us: our situation in life and the demands of our society will clearly show us what these things are.

Then comes concern with intention, with the spiritual intensity with which we are to do our work.

Finally, for every work in the world there is a correct way of carrying it out: it is the latter which must be made part of the religious spirit in our time, so that we are

not accused of replacing technique with piety, of throwing holy water on inadequately done tasks. Only in this way can we give substance to our love of God, and it is thus that the world will return to His will. The world will then cease being profane, an autono-

mous "nature" in which man may work as he wants to work, an autonomous civilization of which man is the creator. On the other hand, piety will take on a seriousness which it has lost to some extent by being acosmic and puritanical; it will once again plunge itself into the world of matter and history.

SAINTS OF THE EXCEPTIONAL WAY

Our Permanent Corrective

We have been dealing in this work with possible characteristics of a new type of saint: we have been describing a model. There are dangers involved in this kind of projection and it is a good to keep clearly in mind what these dangers are. We have said that the saint will respond to demands of his daily life as a way of expressing his love for God; this emphasis on work can lead to mere activism, to mere involvement in a situation for its own sake. As for thoughts of love, these might be debased into rationalization, a sort of guarantee of the action in which we are immersed. It is the same with what was said of intention: it can lose its purity and even its sincerity and turn into a type of self-righteousness.

Such errors are compounded with misunderstanding if the sense of responsibility for the world degenerates into thoughts of inevitable progress and unguarded optimism. The basis of the Christian life is the Cross, and it would be foolish to think of ourselves living the Christian life without some share in the suffering of Christ. Our whole attitude would become nothing else than a naturalism preoccupied with the world and the work of the world.

In dedicating ourselves to the work of the world, we can also forget the significance of detachment from the immediate ties of the world: observe the warning given by St. Paul that "the time is short; it remains that those who had wives be as if they had none; and those who weep, as though not weeping; and those who rejoice, as though not rejoicing;

and those who buy as though not possessing and those who use this world as though not using it" (1 Cor. 7:29-31), and that of St. John, still more urgent: "Do not love the world, or the things that are in the world. If anyone loves the world, the love of the Father is not in him; because all that is in the

world is the lust of the flesh, and the lust of the eyes and the pride of life; which is not from the Father but from the world. And the world with its lust is passing away, but he who does the will of God abides forever." (1 Jo. 2:15-17)

We thus return here to the permanent significance for any kind of Christian sanctity of the saints of the exceptional way: the men and women who, for love of God, sacrificed all, dared all, undertook to bear every suffering and pain for God. They shall remain for all the ages of Christianity to the end of the world the proper guides to spur on our efforts; as models who will inspire our slackening efforts. At the heart of their ideal of sanctity was the faithful achievement of the evangelical counsels: poverty, chastity, obedience. They undertook these things to be free for God. And in their freedom we will always be able to see not just something negative, but lessons which will teach us the actual uses of the world: our proper uses of money and property, liberty and community.

The ideal of these saints of the exceptional way will be forever valid. It will teach Christians about the need to establish a suitable order in the uses of property, in free decision, in marriage, and also in all the demands of an authentic culture. In a final analysis that order can be established only in the same spirit, with the same sense of sacrifice and through the same resources by which the great men and women of the exceptional way lived and died.

THE WITNESS OF THE SAINTS

From what has been said up to now, someone might erroneously conclude that the objective of the saints is to provide better solutions to the problems of the world, to render the world just a little more efficient every day. Sanctity in all its mystery upon mystery of grace would be thereby disparaged as just a supernatural means to a totally worldly end. Man would be delivered up to the world as its slave.

The truth is the very opposite. The saints constantly give witness to the ultimate freedom that comes only from Christ. They dedicate themselves earnestly to their tasks in the world because it is God's will for them to know what "history" is — our history, the history of fallen men. It is God's design for them to see how much disorder there is in

man down to his very core, and with how much resistance man opposes God. This is just another way of saying that they experience in their lives the mystery of God's love for man in redeeming man and in giving him his grace.

The hardest part of their experiences is to see that in life there is not only human disorder, but also deliberate and willful disorder, voluntary blindness in the supernatural sphere. Let us merely think of Christ's situation — of the wall of will to power, of blindness, of lying that was erected around Him, and against which His living truth was unable to prevail. It was unable to prevail not because He did not have the power to make it prevail instantly if He so wished, but because He did not want to suppress that freedom by which alone genuine good can be accomplished.

We might even say that this is what happens to all those who wish to do well whatever it is they have to do, even though they might not start from ideas as sublime as that of sanctity. But there is one difference between the Christian and others who simply do their tasks well: the Christian is not permitted ever to despair, ever to be pessimistic even. The Christian does not have the right to say: men are bad, society is corrupt, all effort is without hope. He must simply love the world and remain faithful to it.

He does not love the world in the sense that St. John forbade when he wrote: "Do not love the world, or the things that are in the world" (1 Jo. 2:15). He loves it in the sense which the same Apostle described elsewhere: "For God so loved the world that He gave His only begotten son that those who believe in Him may not perish, but may have everlasting life " (Jo. 3:16). The Christian shares this love of God. Disorder in the world affects him differently than it does the non-believing pessimist who rejects it as corrupt and lost. The Christian, and consequently the saint more than anyone else, suffers with the world in its distress: not because it is his, but because it is the world of God.

Pessimism and optimism are poor ways to come to terms with the conditions of real life. Both of them scorn reality: one finds shelter in the rejection and condemnation of the world; the other in its exultation. But they are both laboring under illusions. The saint, on the contrary, desires only to see the truth, to see the world as it really is.

And the saint perseveres in this faithfulness to the world. They have the strength for this not because they think the world will be "fixed up," if only it is worked at long enough. They are realists and they know that the world can never be "fixed up." The condition of the world is at bottom incurable. It has as its cause the revolt of men against God — a revolt which cannot be eradicated from history, but which can be integrated in a greater love. Nor do the saints always expect to see the results of their efforts; perhaps they will never see any result except failure, must of necessity experience failure, for what they wish for the world is too big ever to be finally and totally achieved before their eyes.

This does not slacken their energy and effort, however, for they know they are part of God's design for the world. If we consider only immediate results, the life of Christ Himself was a defeat, a failure. It ended in a catas-

trophe, and people who listened to him faithfully thought that He Himself perished. But it was precisely by way of that catastrophe that He opened the way of God to the world. The same may be said of saints and of Christians in general. Everything they do has a mysteriously dual character. They concern themselves with caring for the real world and they do so with a sincerity and perseverance greater than those of any reformer; but on the other hand they know that what they do cannot be translated into tangible results. It is simply laid at God's feet to be used in his unknown designs where and how he wishes. Perhaps they will never know anything, never see anything, until the final judgment and the establishment of a new creation.

The saints, strangely enough, feel a greater sense of solidarity than the rest of us with sinners — with those who suffer from contradictions between spirit and body, from anti-social tendencies, from the spirit of rebellion and passion, from deliberate foolishness. They don't just imagine these things to appreciate the plight of the fallen. They have experienced their solidarity with sinners in the doctrines of original sin and they have experienced in their own flesh its transmittal — with the result that the suffering and disorder of the world causes them to feel a personal responsibility for it.

It is true that all Christians feel this solidarity in some measure, but it generally remains at an unconscious level. Here again the saints are realists. They do not try to hide themselves from the truth. They face up to it. While we others are aware only under certain circumstances of original sin, they live it constantly. And that makes them reach a depth of suffering with others and for others to a degree that there is no longer any question of their need to see immediate success; they enter into union with the suffering which Christ suffered for the world. Quite simply put, the path of sanctity consists in wishing to do at each moment what is good. But how many of us know what is good?

Doesn't it often happen that the interplay of various factors makes our vision unclear? We ought then to postulate the following: when you wish to know what you must do, you must be prepared to see it; and to do it, as soon as you have seen it. The road to such disposability is undoubtedly a long one. One is almost tempted to say that it has no end; for behind each single resistance overcome, do not fresh ones without end rise up?

Sometimes the confusion is so great that we do not even manage to ask what is good. Sometimes, we seem to see not evil confronting good, but good confronting good, so that we are thence reduced to satisfying ourselves with probabilities, or remaining in a situation without solution. We can get the impression in these circumstances that the search for the good is a hopeless battle. All those who labor in the real world are aware of the resulting anguish.

And yet, we must not give up. The word 'tragic' does not suffice to express the nature of the life which we have in this world. The loss of good people from the Church, the big opportunities missed, the failure of projects to achieve something perfect: these are just so many dismal and discouraging signposts of life. But here again, whoever has a Christian outlook will not seek refuge in excuses and ideologies; he must "hope against hope," believe (Rom. 4:18) and for the rest call upon the justice of God.